This book belongs to

Snowflakes

A Coloring Book for Adults

Joelle B. Burnette

Don't Sweat It...Call a

There's only one rule...Have fun! These coloring pages are here for your pleasure. The designs in this book are top-bound to accommodate both left- and right-handed artists. Regardless of your skill level, there is no wrong way to color these designs.

Whether you're in the darkness of winter or sitting on a sunny beach, get in the mood for coloring the snowflakes by listening to Joelle's favorite

 holiday songs in her special **Spotify playlist, "Making Spirits Bright."** This playlist, at **http://bit.ly/SnowflakesMusic,** includes more than five hours of music.

Now, turn on some music, relax, and have fun. Here are some suggestions to make your coloring experience more enjoyable:

Tips

In the back of the book, you will find some swatch pages. Use those snowflakes to test your colors and see how they look on the page. Keep track of your favorite colors by noting their names in the provided space.

When working on a drawing, protect the next page by inserting a loose piece of paper between the two, or cut the designs out of the book before starting your coloring.

Flaunt Your Flakes

Everyone creates art from their own perspective, and Joelle would love to see your interpretation. Please share your finished work in a book review where you made your purchase, at the author's Facebook page (facebook.com/Joelle.Burnette.Author), Twitter (@joelleburnette), Intagram (instagram.com/joelleburnette), Pinterest (pinterest.com/joelleburnette), or other social media.

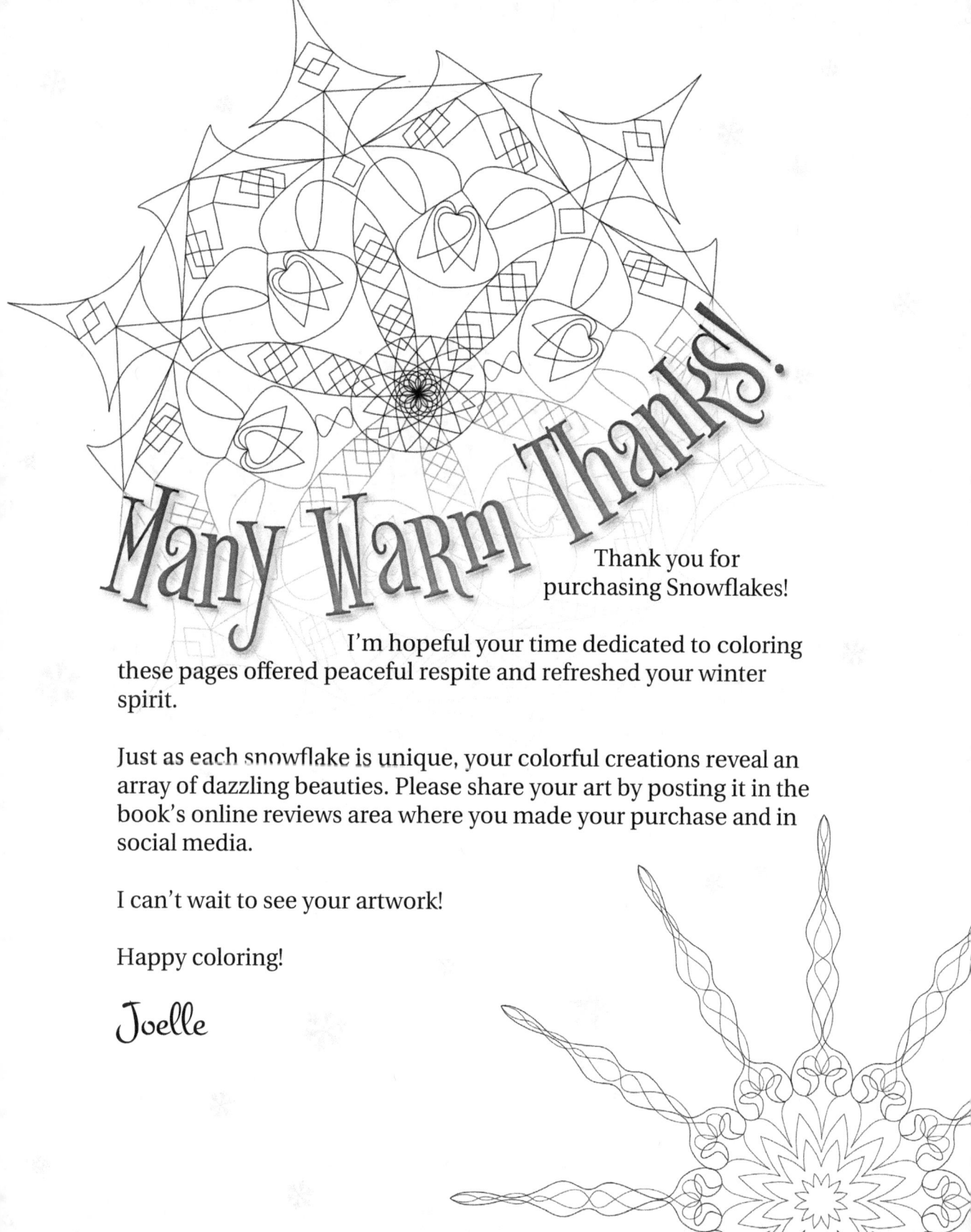

Many Warm Thanks!

Thank you for purchasing Snowflakes!

I'm hopeful your time dedicated to coloring these pages offered peaceful respite and refreshed your winter spirit.

Just as each snowflake is unique, your colorful creations reveal an array of dazzling beauties. Please share your art by posting it in the book's online reviews area where you made your purchase and in social media.

I can't wait to see your artwork!

Happy coloring!

Joelle

About the Author

Joelle Burnette is an award-winning writer and artist, and the author of books including a nonfiction, *Cancer Time Bomb: How the BRCA Gene Stole My Tits and Eggs*, and a children's book, *Freedom Doesn't Just Come Along with a Tree*. Her artwork can also be found in her coloring book *Hearts*. As well, her stories have been published in various anthologies.

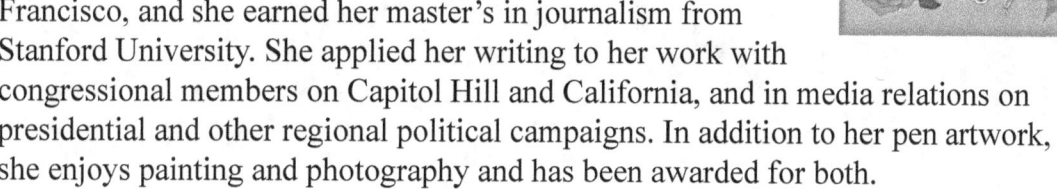

Before writing for a New York Times newspaper in California, Joelle wrote for other newspapers and television news in San Francisco, and she earned her master's in journalism from Stanford University. She applied her writing to her work with congressional members on Capitol Hill and California, and in media relations on presidential and other regional political campaigns. In addition to her pen artwork, she enjoys painting and photography and has been awarded for both.

Connect

❄ Website: JoelleBurnette.net

❄ Facebook: facebook.com/Joelle.Burnette.Author

❄ Instagram: instagram.com/joelleburnette

❄ Twitter: @joelleburnette

❄ Pinterest: pinterest.com/joelleburnette

❄ YouTube: youtube.com/joelleburnette

Color Samples

Keep track of your favorite colors in this quick reference. Fill the snowflakes with your colors. Use the same pen or pencil to write the name of the color on the accompanying line.